How to avoid being

FILTERED OUT

THE WORKBOOK

45 MOST COMMON INTERVIEW QUESTIONS

Peter Botting

All rights reserved. No part of this book may be reproduced or distributed in any form without prior written permission from the author, with the exception of non-commercial uses permitted by copyright law.

No part of this book may be reproduced or transmitted by any means, except as permitted by UK copyright law or the author. For licensing requests, please contact the author at copy@peterbotting.com

All rights reserved. No portion of this book may be reproduced, copied, distributed or adapted in any way, with the exception of certain activities permitted by applicable copyright laws, such as brief quotations in the context of a review or academic work. For permission to publish, distribute or otherwise reproduce this work, please contact the author at copy@peterbotting.com

■ CONTENTS

Foreword ix
Interview coaching feedback x
Thank You xii

TL;DR: What is Filtered OUT - The Workbook? xiii
Thanks (again) for buying Filtered OUT - The Workbook. .. xiii
What is in this workbook? How long will it take to read?. xiii
How does it work? How to use this book?. xv
My Guarantee. If you do the work. xvi
Why is it called Filtered OUT?. xvi
An Inefficient Workbook. Sorry, not sorry.. xvii
Why is it not available in digital format? xvii

Opening up The Interview. 1
Standard, "friendly" opening questions designed to
unpack and assess (or expose) you ... fast

1. Tell us about yourself. 2
2. What brought you here (to us) today? 4
3. Why are you the best person for the job? 6
4. What are your significant achievements to date? What are your proudest (personal/professional) achievements in the past two years? Which of your recent successes have you been most proud of?. ... 8
5. How have you prepared for this interview? 10

Are you right for us? 13
This Industry, This Company, This Job

The Industry. 15
Your knowledge and understanding of the industry;
Your decision to join the industry

6. What do you know about this/our business? Tell us about a business in our sector that is doing well and a business in our sector that is doing poorly? What issues do they both face? Give an example of a company

that you believe has the potential to grow and why? Give an example of a company in our industry that has grown a lot in the last couple of years, and what would you advise them to do next? 16
7. Which other companies did you apply to and why? 18
8. In the last two years, what factors are affecting businesses in this country? Tell me about the broader issues the economy is currently facing. Describe a current issue in the business world What problems do you think (insert industry) businesses face today? 20

The Company 23
Why Us/This Company?

9. Why did you choose to apply to this company? What do you know about us?. 24
10. What are we doing well, and what could we do better? 26

The Job 29
Your match for The Job

11. What do you expect you will be doing during your first year? Describe how you see the role. Are you happy to work weekends and away from home? 30
12. What are your salary expectations? 32

Your Career Path 35
What have you been doing?

13. Talk us through your CV. Why did you choose your course and university? Why did you choose (trade/profession/industry)? 36
14. Do you have any regrets about your choice of career? What would have been your second career choice and why? 38

Managing yourself and those around you 39
Who are you... the real you... what can we expect from you?

Managing Yourself? 41
A British Army Officer gets put on a charge of not performing to standard for getting sunburnt. The rationale is that officers

who aren't disciplined enough to look after themselves can't be trusted to command soldiers. Fair point.

Managing your Career 43
Your ambitions, personal development

15. What are your ambitions for the future? Where do you see yourself in the next five years? 44
16. What new hobby or extracurricular activity have you taken up in the last two years? What have you learnt recently? What book are you reading at the moment? Which is your favourite book? What courses or training (company money/own money) have you done recently? 46
17. Name four role models who influence you/who you would like to meet/favourite dinner guests/are your role models? 48
18. Do you have a mentor? Do you mentor others? 50
19. Tell me about a time you have underperformed or not met your targets; why was this? And what have you learnt from this? 52
20. What is a development area for you? How would you like to address it? How are you handling it? 54
21. What motivates you? 56

Self Awareness, Change and Challenges 59

22. What is the biggest mistake you have made? What did you learn from this mistake? 60
23. What do you consider to be your three biggest strengths and weaknesses 62
24. Do you prefer working from home/hybrid/in the office? Why? 64
25. Tell us about when you have had to overcome a recent challenge/obstacle to succeed and what you have learned about yourself from it. Tell me about a challenging work experience and how you coped/dealt with it. What were the outcomes? 66
26. Tell us about when you had to change plans to complete a project. . . . 68
27. Tell me a time when you had to perform on your own. Do you prefer working in teams or alone? 70
28. Describe an instance where you have had to show adaptability skills. . . . 72
29. How would you keep yourself motivated if your tasks had become a daily routine? 74

Managing People - Leadership 77
The key to climbing the pyramid

30. Tell us about your leadership/management experience. What have you learnt about yourself through being a manager/leader? How have you evolved as a people manager? When you last worked in a team, did you take a leadership position? Why/Why not? 78
31. How do you handle responsibility?. 80
32. Provide an example of how you develop and support inclusivity, equity and diversity in your teams. How do you/will you promote diversity, equality and inclusion? What does diversity mean to you? How would you react if you heard someone say something inappropriate? 82

Managing Up 85
Communicating with your manager - Conflict with the Boss

33. How do you communicate with your boss? Do you make your opinions known when you disagree with the views of your supervisor? How? Give an example of a conflict you had with your superior and how you responded.. 86
34. A senior colleague who recently joined the project team you have been working on was asked to observe you in a presentation you will be making in front of the clients. During the presentation, the colleague questioned your methodology. What would you do?. 88

Managing Pressure and Time 91
Your ability to handle pressure and manage your time

35. How do you deal with working under pressure? When have you worked under pressure? What was the outcome of this pressure situation? How did you cope under pressure? How do you deal with stress? Tell me about a time when you had to meet several competing deadlines. How did you manage this? 92

Managing your Work/Life Balance. 95
Do your job, keep your family happy, and have a third balancing leg

36. How do you switch off on the weekends? - What do you do in your spare time? 96

Managing Customers..**99**
How could you help us attract, look after and retain customers

37. Tell us about a time when you converted a potential client into a client. 100
38. How good are you with customers and managing relationships? Is the customer/client always right?......................... 102
39. Describe an instance when you've had to deal with an angry customer. Give an example of a conflict you had with a customer and how you responded.. 104

Managing Sideways - Teams.............................**107**
Teams, conflicts, challenges, office politics

40. How would you resolve a toxic situation or a turf competition with a team colleague? Tell me a time when you had to accommodate a difference of opinion when working in a team. How did this work out? If a team member disagrees with you, how did you handle that? What was the outcome?.. 108
41. Describe a time when you worked in a team. What was your role in the team? How would you describe yourself as a team member?....... 110
42. Tell us about when you navigated office politics... what happened, what did you do, and how it worked out?.................. 112

Closing down The Interview............................**115**
Time to reassure, consolidate or rescue the interview

43. Is there anything we have missed that you wish we'd asked you? What do you wish we had asked you?............................ 116
44. Do you have any questions for us?......................... 118
45. How would you like us to remember you?................... 122

Elon Musk's Two Interview Questions...................**125**

46. "Tell me the story of your life. And the decisions that you made along the way and why you made them."........................ 126
47. "... tell me about the problems (you've) worked on and how (you've) solved them.".. 128

Conclusion 130

■ FOREWORD
MARK MASON

Peter knows what he wants to say, he says it clearly and then he moves on to the next point. At every stage of this book you are learning something new, and learning it well.

If you stay as focused as the book is, you'll go far.

■ INTERVIEW COACHING FEEDBACK

"I was invited to join the partnership! Which of course I accepted! It was an incredible feeling, with a flood of relief and excitement. It has been a fantastic few days - tomorrow is officially my first day as a partner.

My wife and I discussed how pleased we are that I spent a day with you and how I needed it to feel in control of the process. The partners who interviewed me said how strong my interview had been. I also wanted to say that the training has helped me enormously in other areas of the job as well."

- Partner, Magic Circle Law Firm

"Peter was an OUTSTANDING and no-nonsense coach. He showed me how to sell my experience at an interview. The interview. For THAT job. Investing in Peter's coaching obviously worked because I was successful and am absolutely over the moon with my new role. He also guided me through the process of negotiating my salary up which saw an increase of over 35%. I would highly recommend using Peter if you are seeking a new role."
- Head of Public Affairs, FTSE 100 company

"Very pleased to say that I have this afternoon been offered the job. Thanks for your help, it really was invaluable!

- General Counsel, U.K. National Regulatory Agency

"From over five thousand applicants I was offered one of twenty places at a top 3 consulting firm and couldn't be happier. Without Peter's help, it's unlikely I would have made it through the first round. I would recommend Peter to any graduate who wants to achieve their very best in their interviews."

- Graduate, Top 3 Consulting Firm

"It's official, I can't thank you enough for all your help and support!."

- Partner, Top 3 Consulting Firm

"Thank you Peter. Very good thinking. You are so sneaky. You deserve the bonus we agreed!"

- DG, Global Agency

■ THANK YOU

Thank you to YOU - for buying this book. I know it will help you be better prepared for the interview process. Tell me how and where you use it and how your career is going and if you have any suggestions for improvements. My contact details are on the last page.

A huge thank you to my eye-rolling long-time consiglieri Liam for getting the final version formatted and uploaded to Amazon and turning my words into what is now in your hand.

Thank you to Greg, Mark, Liz, Lukas and Jakob for taking the time and effort to read my original draft and give me their blunt, and therefore hugely useful, feedback. Feedback is my favourite word. I give out feedback freely as part of my coaching. Honest feedback is rare and something my clients value. These friends gave me large buckets of it back. The final version is so much better because of their input. It's imperfect because of me.

Thank you to Mark for his wonderful foreword. Mark is a professional writer as well as reviewing books - his words dropped my jaw. His suggested edits improved this book.

Thank you to Lukas for refreshing the design of the original Filtered OUT book.

TL;DR: WHAT IS FILTERED OUT - THE WORKBOOK?

Fact: You will fail your interview if you can't handle the common and predictable questions guaranteed to appear in every interview. This book helps you do that. You don't just read it. You write in it. Your answers. Not mine. It's a WORKbook. YOUR workbook. Get it?

This isn't the prettiest book you'll ever own. But once you've written in it, and made it yours, it will be your companion for every job interview.

THANKS (AGAIN) FOR BUYING FILTERED OUT - THE WORKBOOK.

This is a companion workbook to "How to avoid getting Filtered OUT". Both books work as standalones, so you don't need to read one before the other or to have read one to make sense of the other. It would be much better for you (and a little bit better for me, obviously) if you bought both - together they cost less than three drinks in London money or one cocktail in NYC money - but you don't HAVE to. But you should...

If you knew I have a 30-year career coaching people for interviews and we met in a pub or a cocktail bar, you would ask my advice on an interview you had coming up. Wouldn't you? And you'd buy me a drink or two, wouldn't you? That would be fair.

This book, Filtered OUT - The Workbook, has nearly 13,000 words of me in it, and Filtered OUT has over 18,000 words of me in it... so that must be worth three drinks, huh? Buy the books. It's your career we're talking about here. Your stories.

WHAT IS IN THIS WORKBOOK? HOW LONG WILL IT TAKE TO READ?

Many "interview" books, online articles and videos focus on "tough interview questions". They are great for internet clickbait headlines but are no use at all if you are never asked those bizarre, smartarse questions in YOUR interview. Why waste your limited time prepping for something which might (maybe/possibly/could) come up when you need to focus on the questions that WILL come up?

This book's job is not to prepare for a winning smash (I like tennis and used to be a tennis coach), although good answers to these questions could do that. I designed this book to help you prevent being filtered out (geddit?) by your unforced errors. To stop you screwing up. If you reduce or eliminate unforced errors, you can still win a match even if you botch an occasional tricky shot or question.

This workbook has 45 of the most commonly used interview questions encountered by my clients at all levels, from fresh graduates to business leaders at or near the C-suite. Plus 2 cool questions that Elon Musk uses which I would use if I was hiring!

The questions include some of their versions or derivatives. It's not exhaustive (how could it be?), but you'll be a damn sight better prepared if you complete this book properly.

If you thoughtfully (!) consider and then write out your answers to all of these questions, then review and edit them - you will know more about yourself, have a huge confidence burst and enter any interview process more calmly and with significantly enhanced clarity of thought.

I do not give you "perfect answers" or sample answers. I outline my thoughts on their rationale for asking the question and some ideas to trigger and focus your thinking when you draft your answers. While my interview coaching is tailored to the client, this book is trying to help a variety of people at different stages in their careers and with their unique life stories to formulate their answers. Your answers. This will be your unique book when you have completed it. Guard it and keep it safe for your next interview and the one after that! It's your interview workbook.

I want to help you push the interviewer's buttons by avoiding crappy copy-and-paste answers, which so many people regurgitate to the frustrated eye-rolling of the interviewers.

This book is perfect for your rucksack or bag so you can work with it anywhere. Work on it during your lunch break. On the bus. In the train. In a cafe. Or pub.

But while this book has been years in the making and weeks in the writing, it will take you time to complete the workbook too - if you take it seriously. Do the maths: 47 questions at a minimum of 200 words an answer - that's nearly 10,000 words. I take about an hour to complete good 500 words on a good day (I write slowly, and I'd be sacked as a journalist within weeks!). You theoretically need at least 12 really concentrated hours to complete the book. Reality: you will need more. But hey…What else are you doing this week?

HOW DOES IT WORK? HOW TO USE THIS BOOK?

It works when you work. If you do the work.

You read a question. You think about what I have written. You think about your personal story. You write in your answer. Ideally, in pencil, so you can come back and review and edit it. Old school techniques, I know.

Using a pen or pencil and paper also helps you clarify your thinking and remember far better than digital does - it has a big "sticky memory" advantage over digital work: writing by hand anchors things in your head. Plus, we're lazy, and when writing by hand, we only put in the relevant words and sentences and not the fluffy guff we speak or type.

Delete lazy cliches that have lost their colour and expand on unsubstantiated claims. Only deploy words that will actually help perform the mission - the mission is to survive the question or win points with your answer and to differentiate yourself from the other contestants for the job. Please note my deployment of the word deployed. A deployed word has a mission. We often (usually!) speak thoughtlessly, throwing words around without a purpose. Words without a defined mission are just noise.

Then you do the next question. There are 47. How long it takes you to work through - that is up to you. YOU have to do the work!

Did I mention it was a WORKbook?

MY GUARANTEE. IF YOU DO THE WORK.

Working through this book will stop you from being self-indulgent with your answers. It will help you be more disciplined, write with purpose, and differentiate yourself from your competitors.

Do I guarantee you will win every interview after you do the work? Of course not, but you'll screw up less. Much less. And if you have filled in every page and been unsuccessful at ten first-level interviews (and can prove it!) - email me, and we'll do a deal on some coaching.

Some of the questions are asked in different ways - I have given you some of those variations. They are the same question asked in different ways and deserve the same answer - possibly tweaked a bit. I've done this rather than listing them separately - which would just add more paper and make the book cost more. Which would be dumb and dull.

Don't get bored with all these predictable questions. Pity the poor interviewers who definitely DO get bored with them. Instead of being bored - be happy the questions you've prepared for in this workbook have come up. Then stand out by delivering your interesting thought-through answers to their boring questions.

Expect the unexpected. Bored interviewers might ask something random simply to alleviate their boredom - smile and embrace the random as something you anticipated. The stories and prep you do for these questions will give you loads of potential ammunition, which may help you to answer any random questions.

WHY IS IT CALLED FILTERED OUT?

The first book is called "How to avoid being Filtered OUT". You can buy that too, if you want - it's on Amazon. This book is called "Filtered OUT - The Workbook". Their jobs are the same. To stop you from being filtered out during the interview process. Getting a job is easy. On paper. All you have to do is never be filtered out - you just need to get to the next stage of the interview process. The last person standing gets the job.

AN INEFFICIENT WORKBOOK.
SORRY, NOT SORRY.

There are 47 predictable questions here - including some of their variations or derivatives. These are questions likely to come up, but they won't all be asked in every interview. So in that sense, it's inefficient.

I want you to have a nearly* full armoury of thought-through answers. Being over-prepared is always better than being under-prepared.

*fully prepared doesn't exist.

WHY IS IT NOT AVAILABLE
IN DIGITAL FORMAT?

Because I want you to win interviews and stop being Filtered OUT far more than I want to sell unused digital products that clutter up your phone. Because you can't write in a digital book with a pen or pencil. Please go back and reread "How to use this book."

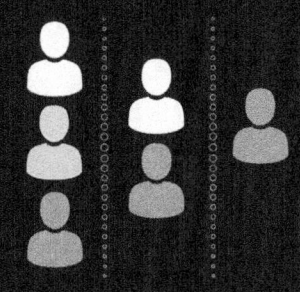

OPENING UP THE INTERVIEW

Standard, "friendly" opening questions designed to unpack and assess (or expose) you ... fast

1

Tell us about yourself.

This question is a magical opportunity for you and is a frequently used, brilliant opening. Why? Because it's effectively: "Give the candidate 3-5 minutes without any guidance or safety rails - what will they do with it?" Your answer to this question could filter you out, keep you in the process or make you stand out.

It's easy to answer this question badly - like writing a rubbish Tinder profile that lists job titles and interests. But it's also a great - and predictable - opportunity for you to sell yourself and stand out. And avoid being filtered out!

This question is your chance to give a crafted summary of you and your skills, qualifications and experience - tailored for this company based on the Job Description and your research.

They want to hear an idea of who you are, a taste of your personality and an understanding of what drives you, how you work and approach things, what this drive has achieved, what you have learned, and what you bring to their table. So don't be dull, don't give a list of titles or qualifications and don't be unresearched. (That is a word now, OK? Don't be it!)

2

What brought you here (to us) today?

Now is an excellent time to point out that you must listen carefully to the question asked. Questions 1, 2 and 3 are all very similar but formulated slightly differently. Although your answer will cover the same ground, it should focus on the question asked. Some people answer Question 3 instead of the answer to this question or Question 1.

There's a difference between why you want this job and why you would be good at it. "Why should we hire you?" should trigger a response that covers both.

Some people unconsciously make the mistake of conflating all of these questions and answering all these questions with one answer but no clarity of thought. Conflating is only okay if done consciously with clarity of thought, precision and intent.

N.B. I am fully aware I used the phrase clarity of thought twice in the last paragraph. Not apologising. Clear thinking leads to clear communication.

This question should include your backstory, skills and experience, as well as your future ambitions and why the combination of the two makes you and them a match.

3

Why are you the best person for the job?

This is a similar question to Question 1, "Tell us about yourself", but it's a lot more focused on why you would be immediately useful and add value - filling their immediate needs. That means comparing your skills, ability, knowledge, and experience with the job description. Remember, though while organisations look for people to fill gaps immediately, they also look for future potential. You should aim to create in their mind a reassuring and convincing mental image or video of you doing the advertised job and your future potential.

Trigger their imagination about what value you could add in the short, medium and long term. Show you can fix their immediate problem and have the ambition and the potential for bigger-picture stuff in the future.

4

What are your significant achievements to date? What are your proudest (personal/professional) achievements in the past two years? Which of your recent successes have you been most proud of?

All these question derivatives should trigger the same plug + play answer. Lists are never a good answer to a question - especially not this one.

Successes might be getting to university, resolving people-management issues, engineering breakthroughs, or sports achievements. Whatever it is, it needs a narrative and a story. It must have involved focus and effort and be meaningful to you. If you're not beaming at the end of the story and able to explain the essential ingredients to the challenge you faced, the choices you made, and what you learned about yourself, you haven't done your job.

If it was part of a team, share the credit generously - do not be greedy. Taking credit for the work of others will be a red flag to a thinking organisation.

This answer indicates how you would face challenges in the future and can be an interview winner for you.

How have you prepared for this interview?

The interviewer wants to know what they asked. They want to see whether you have prepared for the interview and, if so, how. But there is another reason for asking this question.

Some say this is to find out how badly you want the job, but the purpose of the question is more intelligent than that cheap negotiating tactic - although such things exist. It aims to discover more about you and how you go about things. Are you somebody who wings it with projects, deadlines and routine work? Are you thorough and a planner?

Have you conducted research for this interview, invested in interview coaching, taken the day off to prepare, made sure you got enough sleep, travelled the route to the interview from home or checked your Zoom setup?

They may want to know why you have prepared for this interview. Have you realised or been made aware of mistakes you have made in other interviews that you have since addressed, or are you just diligent, and that is how you go about things - or a combination?

Honesty is always the best policy. (Not just for this question but for all questions.) Especially when it comes to your CV and qualifications. It is (more than) ok to acknowledge your fear of underselling yourself at interviews or the fact that you sometimes get nervous (who doesn't?), or that you haven't had an interview recently or perhaps have never had an online interview.

Admitting to a weakness and explaining how you've addressed it proves that you are self-aware, a problem solver and open to learning. If you've invested money and time in yourself, you will be rare, stand out and be in demand.

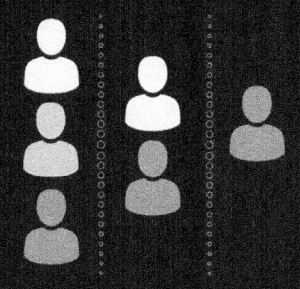

ARE YOU RIGHT FOR US?

This Industry, This Company, This Job

This sequence of questions is obvious - or at least it should be. If you apply for a job in an industry and have no interest or belief in that industry - in its purpose or WHY - then you will lose to an identical candidate who is interested in that industry and demonstrates that. Even the most mercenary boss inwardly wants you to believe in their official narrative. They also think you will be a harder-working and more committed team member.

You have spent so much time and effort getting an interview it is crazy not to research the industry, the company itself and anything you can find out about the job.

It doesn't matter whether your career is industry specific or in a (relatively) industry-agnostic career path like HR or Finance - you are underselling yourself if you don't do the prep.

■ ■ ■
THE INDUSTRY

Your knowledge and understanding of the industry; Your decision to join the industry

6

What do you know about this/our business? Tell us about a business in our sector that is doing well and a business in our sector that is doing poorly? What issues do they both face? Give an example of a company that you believe has the potential to grow and why? Give an example of a company in our industry that has grown a lot in the last couple of years, and what would you advise them to do next?

One of this cluster of questions is virtually guaranteed and is in the same probability level as "Tell us about yourself?"

I have left this group of questions separate from the following question because they are industry and business-focused and so granular. The next question is at a higher altitude - this question demands in-depth or insider knowledge (and jargon) of businesses in your industry. To be able to answer this, you need to be all over the trade publications relevant to your industry.

They ask this to see if you are cloaked in industry knowledge or whether you still need to do your research, which shows a pitiful lack of interest and damages your chances.

Which other companies did you apply to and why?

This is a tricky question. Particularly if they ask whether you have an interview with their competitor and how far you are in the process. Too many possibilities to cover here in much detail. However…

Honesty is always the best policy - but that doesn't mean you have to tell everybody everything. I would summarise why you like the industry and disclose who you chose to apply to within that industry but be coy about timelines and progress with interview processes - unless it is valuable and relevant to getting an actual offer on the table or negotiating up an offer. Which is not at the first interview stage!

8

In the last two years, what factors are affecting businesses in this country? Tell me about the broader issues the economy is currently facing. Describe a current issue in the business world What problems do you think (insert industry) businesses face today?

If you are applying for a cog-in-the-wheel entry-level job and know this, it will help you stand out from your competitors - in a good way. At any higher level, not knowing this will make you stand out - in a very bad way. The only way to stand out here will be by having a more thoughtful and insightful perspective on the question than your competitors.

Why do they ask this? Showing spatial awareness and a helicopter-altitude perspective of how life, the economy, your industry and this business will be affected will mark you as having potential for higher management ranks. It also tests whether you are curious and stay informed and up-to-date on current affairs and business news.

Some say that research is vital AND that you can do this the night before. I disagree. There is too much to absorb in a short period - plus you have other work to do. You need to inhale news about the economy, politics and industry regularly. Daily updates on what is happening are the essence of being informed on your industry and current affairs. Using digital subscriptions to respected financial, political and trade press publications in your country will help you stay up-to-date and able to answer this. In the U.K. I recommend The Spectator for current political affairs (their superb Portrait of the Week is staccato and commentary-free) and the FT for business news.

THE COMPANY

Why Us/This Company?

Why did you choose to apply to this company? What do you know about us?

If you haven't researched the company, you are dumb. This is standard stuff. They want an insight into how diligent (see: due diligence) you are.

But don't be superficial: research the company, the website, social media accounts, and recent speeches by the CEO or Managing Partner. Closely examine the job description and their blurb about themselves for what they are looking for and any information you can find about what they value and characteristics they prize. These may be both stated and unstated - sometimes, what is really relevant to them is not written down, so be prepared to research and tread between the lines. Read what others say about them in the relevant trade press. Check out what Twitter says and read all the internet news items on them, going back a few pages.

Talk about the challenges they face and why these interest and motivate you. Do talk about the opportunities for career progression. Do talk about their ambitions for the future and how those align with yours.

Don't talk about the benefits or the salary. Focus on why you match the purpose and ethos of the company (read their website!), how you could help the company succeed, what past achievements you could potentially replicate for them, and how you would fit into the company's culture.

Company cultural fit is worth mentioning - scoring well here is a key decider after your tech or business skills are established.

10

What are we doing well, and what could we do better?

This should be a relatively easy question if you have done the research well, that I outline in Question 15. They are asking to check the depth of your research to understand how well you frame negative feedback and possibly in an honest quest for information from fresh eyes.

Be careful how candid you are. Do not lie but be careful. You want to get to the decision-maker - your focus until getting to the decision-maker is NOT to be filtered out. If the decision maker is C-suite, you can be more candid at that stage - because those people usually* get there by listening to feedback and have an appetite for it.

*I did say usually! It's not always the case!

THE JOB

Your match for The Job

11

What do you expect you will be doing during your first year? Describe how you see the role. Are you happy to work weekends and away from home?

This is a solid expectation management and research-focused question. They are testing to see if you have done any research, and there are many ways you can find out about the day-to-day realities of the job. What will your typical day look like? Project or routine? Learning or doing? Responsibilities? Who will you answer to? Office-based, home or travel?

Apart from assessing your research, they want to manage your expectations. They want to reduce unwanted churn of recruits, which means mutual honesty. The job may well be (unless you're very fortunate) sometimes dull and routine - that's sadly part of being an adult.

The internet is your friend for industry discussion boards and job descriptions, but you can also ask people in that industry. If you don't know anyone like that, use LinkedIn to find someone who is, send them a message and ask them. They will often be disarmingly honest and may even become a mentor or flag up opportunities. Who doesn't like someone who shows initiative?

12

What are your salary expectations?

They are checking to see if you are being realistic or wasting their time. They also want to know whether you are affordable, whether they can meet your expectations on this important topic and whether you are good at selling yourself. How can they expect you to sell them and represent them if you can't sell yourself?

Your industry and company research should help you answer this, but a definite numerical answer will kill you here. This question should include a mini sales pitch which summarises what you bring to the table and demonstrates your knowledge of the market and your understanding of the role and responsibilities of the job. Your answer should be a range based on market evidence rather than a definite figure.

■ ■ ■
YOUR CAREER PATH

What have you been doing?

13

Talk us through your CV. Why did you choose your course and university? Why did you choose (trade/profession/industry)?

This is not a reading exercise. They want to know what you have done in your career and why. Most people, including me, have stumbled into their current positions by chance (possibly based on a chance opportunity or advice from family, a teacher or a mentor) so not having had a plan from the age of 12 isn't bad. In fact, with the current pace of technological change, having had a plan at that age should probably be certifiable.

They want to know whether there are common themes or threads or consistency in your choices, about your prior experience, and what skills, experience, insight and self-awareness you would bring to the table.

Focus enthusiastically on the learning and career opportunities, the future and developing yourself. Avoid the monetary aspect, WFH, or flexible work hours - unless the latter is key to your circumstances and choices.

14

Do you have any regrets about your choice of career? What would have been your second career choice and why?

This is an excellent opportunity:

- To prove that you have chosen them and their industry rather than applying for any old job
- To show that you have reflected, are self-aware and have learnt things about yourself
- Which allows you to show them a different side to you they otherwise might not have known about (from your cover letter, application, CV, or interview), which makes you more attractive.

Regrets: this may be because of a lack of information at the time, a bad experience or because technological advancements or other changes have affected your career or disrupted your industry. Importantly, what have you done about this? Have you broadened the scope of your role, developed yourself and studied in your spare time?

Second career choice: Do not simply say - "I wanted to be a pilot". Explain why you want the job and career you are interviewing for, and why you wanted to be a pilot. Explain your motivations for both your industry and career choices, how you approached the decision, and why you made the decision you did.

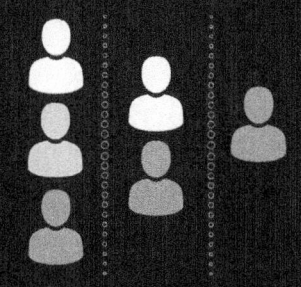

MANAGING YOURSELF AND THOSE AROUND YOU

Who are you… the real you… what can we expect from you?

■ ■ ■
MANAGING YOURSELF?

A British Army Officer gets put on a charge of not performing to standard for getting sunburnt. The rationale is that officers who aren't disciplined enough to look after themselves can't be trusted to command soldiers. Fair point.

MANAGING YOUR CAREER

Your ambitions, personal development

15

What are your ambitions for the future? Where do you see yourself in the next five years?

You need to have a plan. We all need a plan. To have a plan, we also need a goal. Plans and goals change as life happens and opportunities arise. So your plan will almost certainly be massively edited or thrown overboard at some stage. But identify a goal first and then map your plan to get there.

If you're applying for your first job, you have a blank sheet of paper. If you're 20 and have a 20-year plan, you might be justifiably called weird. Far worse if you haven't taken action on it yet. Jobs and careers today exist that didn't exist when you were born, and there will be new ones within the next ten years. But having a direction is a good start.

If you already have a career and want to progress, you already have an idea of the goals, stages, strategies and plans ahead.

But a plan is not enough - what action have you been taking, what progress have you made, what investment have you made, what traction have you achieved?

16

What new hobby or extracurricular activity have you taken up in the last two years? What have you learnt recently? What book are you reading at the moment? Which is your favourite book? What courses or training (company money/own money) have you done recently?

Many people of all ages simply don't have an answer to any of the variants of this type of question without lying. Life may have gotten in the way, or they are just happy with their thing and routine, or they are just a bit dull.

Being in your 30s, 40s or 50s doesn't mean you cannot learn new things - they may not be sports or hobbies - they may be technical qualifications, languages or skills.

The Germans have a wonderful saying: "As soon as you become a master at one thing, you should become an apprentice at something else."

Companies like to claim they are learning organisations (and some are), so it is on brand for them to hire people who fit their brand.

So if you are one of those who would have to lie if asked this question, start learning something new today. Reading this book is a start. Books are great - but take ages to read - I prefer summaries. TED and TEDMED are great learning platforms. You can learn more about just about anything on YouTube. LinkedIn offers skills courses, and EDX.org offers impressive online courses.

17

Name four role models who influence you/ who you would like to meet/favourite dinner guests/are your role models?

What they are looking for here is not just four names. You should have these names ready in all variables - dead, alive, this industry, fantasy, Hollywood/fiction. You shouldn't have to play for time. This is a no-brainer, predictable question that should be prepared for and thought through. But there's more…

You should have reasons why you would like to meet these four names. These reasons should spotlight the strengths/characteristics/skills/features/abilities/accomplishments they possess and are relevant to you because you have them. Or aspire to, admire or are working towards them.

Admiring something is not good enough. You need to prove you are working towards it because you've identified it as desirable, acknowledged you have a gap, and have taken or are taking action. Tell the interviewer how you are going about bridging that gap.

18

Do you have a mentor? Do you mentor others?

If you're neither of these, you should be. At least one. Ideally both. Think of mentors as your private Non-Exec Directors, just as a business has Non-Exec Directors who act as a council of elders. These people aren't involved in the day-to-day business but are there as guides and advisers.

Maybe they have industry or career-relevant experience - the main thing is that they are disinterested and dispassionate professionally. They don't have an agenda, they are interested in your success, and you trust them to be honest with you - often brutally so, in the way that friends and families sometimes are not.

Mentors give you perspective and guidelines and help you refocus, shift gears or even redirect your activities. They want you to take risks carefully and may have advice on what to avoid or what is possible - two things you may not see.

Ed Johnson, CEO and Co-Founder of PushFar, the world's leading mentoring platform, says:

> "A mentor is vital to career success. They provide important alternative perspectives, insights and knowledge, often from a place of first-hand experience. They've usually been where you are now, faced the challenges you are facing and achieved the goals you hope to also achieve."

But it works both ways. Mentors can benefit as much from mentoring as mentees do from being mentored.

Mentoring means articulating and clarifying thoughts and ideas in a way that does not judge or patronise and benefits both parties.

There's no downside to mentoring or being mentored. It doesn't matter how little you think you know - there will always be people who know less and need a mentor. Pass on the good karma.

19

Tell me about a time you have underperformed or not met your targets; why was this?
And what have you learnt from this?

Honesty is not just a good policy - it's refreshing and endearing. If you can claim right now that you've never underperformed or missed your targets, you're a liar, or you've never had challenging targets. I've missed loads of business, sales and delivery targets in my life and let's not even mention the hated writer's deadlines!

What's important here is what you have learned about yourself, time management, building in buffers, and being realistic in terms of time and effort needed.

A reliable person who always delivers on deadlines, targets and projects - no matter what - is a scarce and unusual resource loved by their managers.

20

What is a development area for you? How would you like to address it? How are you handling it?

This is a super question for you because it shows your level of self-awareness. It shows that you have reflected not just on yourself or those around you. It shows that you are ambitious and keen to learn and develop. (Please also see Question 16 for platforms where you can start your self-development today).

Having an extra skill or a language could be the deciding factor - or "competitive advantage" - in you getting the job over someone else. I am more interested in people who have experienced different cultures and can speak more than one language.

21

What motivates you?

Have you ever read Maslow's Needs Hierarchy? If you haven't, Google and read it now. We all need the basics - shelter, food, and water. After that, we can address things higher up the pyramid. You could well be in a situation where your priority is finding the money for your rent. Paying the rent and putting food on the table is not to be sneered at - you have no monopoly on this - ordinary people have these issues. You may have been made redundant and need some interim or consultancy work fast to pay the mortgage or the school fees. Look after the basics - again, totally normal.

After addressing these things and life has stabilised - we all start to look up the pyramid. It's a part of the human condition. But different things appeal - power, money, fame, lifestyle, work-life balance, travel, building, and legacy creation.

Answers that annoy most interviewers and me are the generic, and therefore meaningless, answers like "I want to change/improve the world." TO WHAT? These unfocused, plaintive generalisations with no specific goal, plan, or traction are wimpy and thought-free.*

We are looking for your fire, what gets you out of bed. Ideally, this demands skills and expertise that you possess, are good at and are in high demand - and therefore of monetary value.

*4 negative adjectives? Yes. Am aware. I detest that response.

SELF AWARENESS, CHANGE AND CHALLENGES

What is the biggest mistake you have made? What did you learn from this mistake?

Another great question you should welcome. No matter how bad the mistake and how much of a life-changing disaster it feels at the time, and I've seen and done some big ones, all mistakes help you learn, get stronger and develop - if your approach and your attitude allow this.

Once the desire to fall into a black hole has diluted and time has given you perspective, and the disaster hasn't happened or it happened and you survived, then the true value of the mistake can be realised.

You should know that everybody makes mistakes all the time - some cover them up or lie about them, some blame others, and some look them in the face and learn from them. Have you never made a mistake? Ever? Then you need to carry more responsibility or take more risks. Not doing these two things is the worst mistake.

What's important is not that you made a mistake; it is how you responded, how you resolved it and what you learnt about yourself. It's reckless and negligent not to fix your mistakes - either on your own or by putting up your hand and asking for help.

23

What do you consider to be your three biggest strengths and weaknesses

Please don't be predictable and dull and talk about how you're so demanding and a perfectionist and quality conscious and that this is an advantage for them because… blah blah…

That's sooooo dull and unoriginal. The good thing for you is that if this is a question for all candidates, you have an excellent opportunity to be different and stand out.

Again, your answers here need to be true. They should also be linked to what your research and the JD say they are looking for. However - don't just claim a list of 3/6 positive expressed and/or implied attributes. Identify and tell the stories for all 6 - so that these attributes are proven. Do that in this workbook and run with whichever appears the most appropriate in the interview. You can also use my headlining technique and then tell the story. If that story resonates, it will trigger a conversation which is good news. They may want to know more about the others. The weaknesses should all be stories that show self-awareness, an eagerness for feedback, an appetite for addressing things and a willingness to learn.

24

Do you prefer working from home/hybrid/in the office? Why?

So much has been written on this. I love coaching from home because it's time efficient and allows me to help clients worldwide - many on the same day. I also like a 9.5-metre commute. But for big-ticket events - there's no replacement for being in the room together.

So why are they asking this? For some employers and employees, it's a dealbreaker, and this question might be a simple filtering information request. Your research of their social media and the job description should tell you their policy.

For various reasons*, a distributed workforce model will remain fully or partially in place for many. So how do you answer this? You should be very honest with your answer question - you may have to live with the consequences! Give your answer and explain why.

*Some advantages and disadvantages of having or being in a distributed workforce:

- Focus on "what" an employee delivers, regardless of gender, location, nationality;
- Access to a more diverse and inclusive global talent pool. Matt Mullenweg, CEO of Automattic (WordPress & Tumblr), spoke at TED. He believes that "talent and intelligence are distributed equally throughout the world."
- Increased employee satisfaction, productivity and retention; fewer sick days
- Fewer distractions from colleagues, but what about TV, your family or the fridge?
- Reduces/avoids commuting time and fuel and allows a better work/life balance.

25

Tell us about when you have had to overcome a recent challenge/obstacle to succeed and what you have learned about yourself from it. Tell me about a challenging work experience and how you coped/dealt with it. What were the outcomes?

This question is doing a lot of heavy lifting. No wonder it is one of Elon Musk's favourite interview questions. (See question 47 after you have answered this - in that question he has a slightly different focus.)

Interviewers ask this question to understand your problem-solving and decision-making skills, to assess how you communicate and whether you ask for help, as well as determine your resourcefulness, resilience, self-confidence and self-awareness. They want to know how well you cope with pressure.

Tailor your answer and prioritise work-related experiences, but you can also draw on personal experiences like illness or family circumstances that have taught you resilience, resourcefulness, or anything else valuable for a workplace. Emphasise the key soft skills mentioned in the job description.

26

Tell us about when you had to change plans to complete a project.

So what's happened here? Change is a constant in the workplace - this isn't a weird question. Maybe the deadline, scope, focus or definition of the project changed. Maybe the allocated resources, including you, were tasked with an additional project? Perhaps the resources were redeployed, were ill or went on holiday. Whatever happened - it's now up to you to complete the project. What do you do? And what are they really asking or trying to find out?

They want to know how you adapt to changes, how you cope under pressure, and your problem-solving skills.

Pick a time* when something went wrong (it could have been outside your control or because you screwed something up), and you had to embrace the change to complete the project. You may even have initially had a bad response and then corrected it. Just don't blame other people - change happens - it is what it is. To succeed, you must maintain a positive and can-do attitude during the transition - at least most of the time. This should shine through.

*I recommend differentiating yourself using my outcome-focused DARCK+ © storytelling system, which I developed halfway through my 30-year storytelling and interview coaching career. All my clients use this. I want my clients to have a secret weapon that is more comprehensive, tailored, structured and targeted, which takes less time and energy to prepare and, above all, is more potent and effective than anything used by their competitors.

DARCK+ © was built based on what I have learnt while studying and teaching storytelling, including research conducted by a U.S. Academic commissioned by DARPA.

27

Tell me a time when you had to perform on your own. Do you prefer working in teams or alone?

Nobody wants to have to tell somebody what they should do every minute of every day. You're also not a 12-year-old who can't do anything without your best friend. They're looking for somebody who can carry out projects independently - but what does that mean? Your answer should illustrate your ability to work independently and on your own initiative without being told what to do. Describe how you approach working alone, how you pull in help if needed, how you keep motivated, focused and on track, keep to deadlines and maintain quality.

Tell about the results and what you have learnt about yourself, how to manage your time, stay disciplined, and improve.

One of my mentees was hired by his dream employer after interning for them. When they hired him, they explained that they had never had to tell him anything twice and "...everything we gave you to do, you did". For them, and most managers, these two things are remarkable. Wow! How easy is it for you to stand out?

28

Describe an instance where you have had to show adaptability skills.

Interviewers ask this question to see how you adapt to different or shifting work environments - key for work involving travel, projects, or work in varied settings.

Adaptability is a crucial skill valued by employers because it shows a positive, open-minded ability to embrace the unknown. They want somebody who can adapt fast and appropriately to new circumstances.

Some jobs are routine and won't change much. That's ok. But unusual things still happen, and you need to show that you can handle disruptions and unexpected changes thrown at you - even if they are not what you routinely expect.

Most job responsibilities do change, and circumstances are constantly changing - so the higher up the pyramid - the more the winds of change will buffet you. You need to be able to describe such a situation in depth so they are reassured that you can handle change.

29

How would you keep yourself motivated if your tasks had become a daily routine?

You might like a routine work environment and consistently delivering that routine work is your motivation. That's fantastic. Even better if you are thinking of ways to improve and optimise that routine. The world needs lots of people like you because every business operation relies on people like you turning up every day and doing your routine work brilliantly.

This doesn't mean that you are not creative or inventive. You may focus your creativity on upgrading your work routines or in other spheres of your life.

Others hate routine and crave variety, short-term projects, and excitement. They are motivated by the new and the changing and want to push their boundaries. They want new people, responsibilities, challenges, scenery, and skills. They are also valuable team members - innovation comes from dissatisfaction with the status quo. Senior managers are confronted by change daily, so their jobs are seldom routine.

So there is no wrong or right for you - you are who you are.

This question is aimed at people who do routine work but also have a bit of an itch that needs scratching. If this is you, say so and explain how you go about your work, how you have addressed your aversion to change, and how you keep yourself motivated by upgrading the process involved in your career. Self-awareness is critical here, as is honesty. It's better (unless you need the rent money urgently) to wait for a job that suits your personality.

MANAGING PEOPLE - LEADERSHIP

The key to climbing the pyramid

30

Tell us about your leadership/management experience. What have you learnt about yourself through being a manager/leader? How have you evolved as a people manager? When you last worked in a team, did you take a leadership position? Why/Why not?

Let us ignore here the differences between management and leadership - but follow me on LinkedIn or check my website for articles and posts about this difference. Leadership/management experience is important or even essential to your career progression. But most managers learn on the job initially (which is why many young people experience poor managers). They are only formally trained in either management or leadership once they are reasonably senior.

They want to assess your experience and potential for the future - which means learning and developing this essential people skill. It is ok to speak candidly about what experience you have, what mistakes you have made, what you have learnt, how you have evolved and how management has evolved during your career.

If you are just starting your career or have no management experience, have you had paid or unpaid positions at university, in a sports team, a charity or in your religion?

There are fantastic online courses on LinkedIn and edx.org where you can learn about leadership and develop your knowledge and skills. Do them and talk about them.

31

How do you handle responsibility?

There is a separate conversation about whether you have the agency and the authority to match the responsibility you are given. This question is about whether you assume the authority and step up - whether you've been given the authority or not.

Suppose you work in a start-up or a lean small business where boundaries are blurred. In that case, roles often overlap, there simply isn't enough money or work for a dedicated person for every job, and everybody does everything. In this situation, you can push and expand the boundaries of your job because they want people who step up and earn trust and take on responsibility.

If you are looking for career advancement and promotion, when people start saying, "Oh, she's/he's got this", you're doing well and being noticed. When you start putting up your hand and saying, "I've got this", and then you deliver at the right quality or higher and within the right time frame or sooner, people notice. The short-term "negative" is you will be given more work as they start trusting you more. This is a fantastic opportunity to show that you deliver every time and is a welcome reflection of their growing trust in you.

Managers are at their best when they delegate the outcome, the WHAT, and leave the HOW to you. Assume you have the best managers and step up and do. If you are a manager - describe how you have done this.

Describe how you have assumed or been given responsibility, how you handled it, mistakes you have made, and lessons you have learned - and then applied later in your career.

32

Provide an example of how you develop and support inclusivity, equity and diversity in your teams. How do you/will you promote diversity, equality and inclusion? What does diversity mean to you? How would you react if you heard someone say something inappropriate?

It matters what leaders say. What leaders do matters as much as what they say. Employers want to know your understanding of diversity, equality, and inclusion. Authenticity matters - pick a real example with specific results.

You should go beyond the token, the predictable and the visual and describe your attitudes and approach to advocating, promoting, building and protecting all types of visible and invisible, obvious and not obvious, diversity - including diversity of thought. Diversity of thought is sometimes used as a cop out - you need to demonstrate that you mean it.

They do NOT want a copy-and-paste answer to any questions they ask you - but especially not to this question.

MANAGING UP

Communicating with your manager - Conflict with the Boss

33

How do you communicate with your boss? Do you make your opinions known when you disagree with the views of your supervisor? How? Give an example of a conflict you had with your superior and how you responded.

Managing up is as important as managing down. More so. Whatever position you hold - from CEO down, you always have a boss or bosses. Proactively managing those relationships (plus those with potential bosses and the levels above your current boss) is key to your career success. I am not talking about patronage here - this is also true for fair and merit-based organisations.

That includes being seen as competent and key to their success and the team's performance. But that doesn't mean being a YES person. Good managers want feedback and people prepared to disagree rationally and constructively.

Perceptions and expectations. You need to be seen as competent, your work needs to be visible, and you need to manage the expectations of your boss or bosses. This could be quite political in how you bypass the line of command without creating enemies. Levels above your boss need to be aware of your role and contribution so that while you are boosting your boss's success, they are not taking credit for your work. This is tough when you have an inadequate, insecure or anxious boss.

Your answer depends on what type of boss you have, the situation and politics involved, and the relationship you have actively built with them.

34

A senior colleague who recently joined the project team you have been working on was asked to observe you in a presentation you will be making in front of the clients. During the presentation, the colleague questioned your methodology. What would you do?

This is an interesting question. So let's reread it and do some mental chess or somersaults. Who asked them - you or your boss? Was the presentation in front of the client or during presentation prep? Were they being difficult, clarifying an issue or helping you improve?

Let's assume the worst case. You should have prepared enough not to be thrown off balance. How you respond will reflect well on you with the client, any other members of your team and maybe the questioner.

I would calmly ask them to repeat the question - this calms you, gives you time to think and puts the spotlight back on them. They'll either rephrase, repeat or rethink the question. Answer the rephrased question clearly and then ask them if that was clear. They may pose a further question to which you repeat the procedure. Once they are done, resume your presentation.

The point of putting this question is to remind you to LISTEN and to listen AGGRESSIVELY. It might be a complex question or a series of questions asked as one. Or it might be a badly formulated question. Make notes. With a pen and paper. Think. Ask them to repeat the question if necessary. Do not just grab at the question you think you heard.

Respond almost always beats react.

MANAGING PRESSURE AND TIME

Your ability to handle pressure and manage your time

35

How do you deal with working under pressure? When have you worked under pressure? What was the outcome of this pressure situation? How did you cope under pressure? How do you deal with stress? Tell me about a time when you had to meet several competing deadlines. How did you manage this?

This question comes dressed in many different clothes - but the answer is roughly the same. Tell a story with a dramatic arc (see my website www.peterbotting.co.uk for details); describe how things got hot, what you did and what the results were.

You may have to explain how you usually handle pressure and why you did it differently on this occasion.

Then outline what you learnt from the situation - proving your self-awareness and eagerness to learn. Understanding how you react to pressure, learning from that, and then transitioning to a more effective response is a valuable skill.

Managing competing deadlines by calmly triaging priorities and assessing the importance and urgency of evaluating items in your "in-tray" with competing items with competing time constraints are essential life skills and hugely valuable in a work environment.

A clients who is a senior military officer calls this "kill the crocodile closest to your canoe". Some use the important vs urgent matrix. Some assess in terms of profit vs loss. Others use risk assessments. The important thing is to have a process - handling pressure is a daily reality.

MANAGING YOUR WORK/LIFE BALANCE

Do your job, keep your family happy, and have a third balancing leg

36

How do you switch off on the weekends? - What do you do in your spare time?

This is more than just the avoid-burnout question it appears to be - although being self-aware enough to take care of your energy levels consciously and your work-life balance is super important - for you and them.

Not everyone is a polymath, but people interested in more than one thing are more interesting - that's a fact. A German friend hosts a niece and her husband twice a year for a weekend. By the end of the weekend, she calls me to vent: the husband has only one topic of conversation - his work. She thinks if he visits again, she'll be qualified to do his job.

People who invest time and money in themselves (their leisure activities, relationships and hobbies) are almost always better at doing their job. Their brain is active and stimulated and switches quickly between projects or activities. They are not stuck in a routine or rut, and their actions trigger thoughts that cross-fertilise into other areas.

Their creativity and energy come from the connectivity they get from doing different things. They refuel or sharpen their knife by doing other things rather than overworking or going home after work and couch-slobbing in front of the TV.

MANAGING CUSTOMERS

How could you help us attract, look after and retain customers

37

Tell us about a time when you converted a potential client into a client.

If you can regularly convert potential clients into good-margin, repeat clients, you are almost guaranteed a well-paid job for life and are virtually unsackable. The rainmakers who can bring in customers are critical to every business - whether you are a waiter, a market stall trader, a junior sales executive, an aspiring partner in a professional services firm (law, consulting or accountancy) or a Vice President of a global. Whatever your title - sales is your trade.

Businesses are always looking for people with the potential to increase their profit or bottom line by growing their sales or top line.

There are virtually no business problems that cannot be solved by bringing in more good margin sales. Do this, and you will always be successful.

38

How good are you with customers and managing relationships? Is the customer/client always right?

Wow. Tremendous and connected questions. Retaining a client is as important as attracting a new client. Client retention can become increasingly difficult during a long-term relationship because the honeymoon fades, and they may get bored (because you're not innovating?) and yearn for new.

It often costs a lot of time and money to attract and onboard new clients. Retaining and upselling clients amortises that upfront cost and makes excellent business sense.

In the car industry, the salesperson sells the first car. The service team or the workshop sell the second, third, fourth, fifth cars and the salesperson becomes an order-taker. Which do you think adds the most value? Who has the most demanding job? Tell the story of you doing that job.

39

Describe an instance when you've had to deal with an angry customer. Give an example of a conflict you had with a customer and how you responded.

Stressful situations like this are common, even in the best-run businesses. If you can defuse and resolve these conflicts with finesse, grace, initiative and leadership, you will soon be valued and treated as a fixer by your company.

At the top of the corporate world, this high-stakes situation demands empathy-rich, problem-solving skills. Losing a prominent, high-value client, can severely damage the company's finances and reputation.

It could also get you sacked.

MANAGING SIDEWAYS - TEAMS

Teams, conflicts, challenges, office politics

40

How would you resolve a toxic situation or a turf competition with a team colleague? Tell me a time when you had to accommodate a difference of opinion when working in a team. How did this work out? If a team member disagrees with you, how did you handle that? What was the outcome?

The CEO of a U.S. based client recently told his team and me that the two keys to staying in the company were: being exceptional at doing your job and getting on with other people. Getting on with your colleagues, addressing issues before they fester, and transforming from irritation into hills and then mountains is a crucial career survival/career-enhancing skill.

Being fair-minded and honest about what happened, how you responded, how you communicated and what the outcome was will be such a refreshing and candid contrast to some competitors that you'll stand out positively just for that. Show some lessons learned and a level of self-awareness and humility, and you'll be through to the next round.

41

Describe a time when you worked in a team. What was your role in the team? How would you describe yourself as a team member?

This looks and sounds like Question 40, but it's more of a self-awareness question based on understanding how you contribute to a team.

Do you focus on triggering thoughts, engaging people or getting things done? Good teams comprise all these member types.

You might be the thought trigger, the creative who challenges the team to think of different solutions, presents new ideas and approaches, has specialised skills or inputs, or analyses the team's work, and often plays devil's advocate.

You might engage and include people and represent and chair the team while leading, guiding, listening and opening up participation.

You might be outcome focused and be good at challenging the team to be better, to turn talk into actions and complete projects on time.

People have described me as a useful hand-grenade thrower, facilitator and coach. Allocate me to one of these team types based on your current knowledge of me - easier to do for other people. Now describe yourself.

42

Tell us about when you navigated office politics… what happened, what did you do, and how it worked out?

This sounds like it should be a variation of Question 40. But I have left it separate because of the phrase "office politics". This question is not aimed at everyday colleague competition, communication issues, personality differences, turf battles, etc.

This question refers exclusively to office politics and power plays, and I think it's useful for you to have a different answer. This is because portraying this type of situation and how you responded to or escalated it is incredibly tough without sounding like a crying 12-year-old complaining to a teacher.

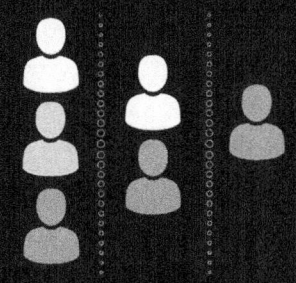

CLOSING DOWN THE INTERVIEW

Time to reassure, consolidate or rescue the interview

43

Is there anything we have missed that you wish we'd asked you? What do you wish we had asked you?

This is a tidy-up question for them and the summarise-emphasise-fix gift question you should be praying for. By now, you should have identified their key drivers and be aware, via your mental checklist, of whether you have ticked those boxes or not.

First, confirm you have correctly identified and understood their key drivers, and give a staccato summary of all relevant areas covered and your "takeaway" messages. Then answer the question with an emphasise-or-fix answer, ideally telling a vivid story with sufficient breadcrumbs to trigger positive and expanding/exploring supplementary questions.

Use this question to ensure their last impression of you is "the full package".

44

Do you have any questions for us?

This is such an easy question to screw up. Let's be clear - by the time they ask you this, they have probably already decided about you. It is almost a courtesy question that they ask to be fair to every candidate. They may not even be listening anymore. You should be able to smell the room by now by their facial and body language, energy levels and use of the future tense rather than the conditional. You could also screw this up by making them change their mind about you from in to out.

There is a better time to start talking about the seller in detail about pensions or bonuses. And it's not now. If you are a YES for them, there is a later stage when such negotiations occur. Negotiation is irrelevant if you are a NO or a MAYBE; they will fob off or evade your question. Use this question to make them reassess you and their verdict of you. You could ask something that helps you survive and progress to the next stage. Remember - that is the goal at every process stage - to get to the next step and NOT be Filtered Out. (Get it?)

This is emergency territory. Time to fix the problem or discover you're out of the running so you can move on.

Change tone and tack. If you've been talking in the past tense about your accomplishments, ask about their future expectations for the job and of the successful candidate. If you've been talking enthusiastically about the job in the future and they look like they're about to throw up, summarise your story briefly (see Question 1) and then be direct and ask: "From what we've discussed so far and what you know about me so far, do you feel I'd be a good fit for the role or do you have concerns I could perhaps clear up?"

A potent question which is easily my favourite: is this: "How will you know in 12 months that you have chosen the right candidate?" This question invariably makes them think and then gives you an opportunity - if you're fast - to provide a tailored version of your answer to Question 1 that proves you would be precisely that candidate. This question makes them, think and visualise you doing the job. It sometimes causes them to redefine their criteria and the role.

Write out your responses for both when things are going well (don't rock the boat) and going badly (how do you get them to retrieve your file from their mental NO pile and reassess you).

45

How would you like us to remember you?

This is a superb opportunity for you, and you should jump for joy if/when they ask you this question. It is usually their last question and much more fun than "Do you have any questions for us" or much easier to prepare for than "Is there anything we missed that you wish we'd asked you?".

You should be dreaming about this question - but how do you answer it?

Answer this with a composite of your answers to questions 1, 2, 3 and 4 - but tweak it to include anything you discovered about their priorities during the interview. You can't know that part yet, so the exercise here is to write a concise and vivid composite of your answers to questions 1-4.

This may well be your closing advert or your closing statement. Ensure they know relevant things you weren't asked or didn't cover. Remind them of all the things you covered that triggered positive feedback.

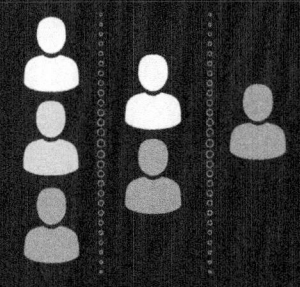

ELON MUSK'S TWO INTERVIEW QUESTIONS

Although Elon Musk says that he interviews based on gut instinct, he does have two interview questions that he asks. I don't know if these are his favourite interview questions or his only interview questions - but they are both demanding questions that I would now use if I was hiring because answers to them reveal so much.

46

"Tell me the story of your life. And the decisions that you made along the way and why you made them."

What is not wanted here? A reading of your CV or a list of your titles.

Musk asks explicitly for three things. The overall story of your life. The decisions you made and your reasoning behind those decisions.

These decisions don't all have to be good ones. Being straightforward about mistakes made and lessons learned is not just endearing and likeable; it also shows an open approach to learning. Learning and an appetite for learning will become increasingly vital as technology upgrades become more frequent.

In many of the earlier questions, I have suggested using stories from within your life chapters in DARCK+© to answer questions. Adopt a broader approach that includes the critical decisions that lead you from one life chapter to the next.

47

"... tell me about the problems (you've) worked on and how (you've) solved them."

Elon Musk:

> "When I interview someone ... [I] ask them to tell me about the problems they worked on and how they solved them. And if someone was the person that solved it, they really will be able to answer at multiple levels - they will be able to go down to the brass tacks. And if they weren't, they'll get stuck. And then you can say, '...oh this person was not really the person who solved it because anyone who struggles hard with a problem never forgets it.'"

Elon explains what he asks and why he asks it, so cheers Elon…but how to answer it? At any middle or senior executive level, you will have worked on problems. They may not be software or engineering problems like Elon and his businesses typically focus on, but they are problems.

I would argue that resolving people and relationship issues within an organisation can be more complex as there are more variables and much more random and unpredictable behaviour.

Whatever path your career has taken, identify a problem or a situation that you have been in charge of fixing - whether you had the official responsibility or not - and describe the situation and how you went about it in detail.

Then go one step further and ask someone to read it and give you the most obvious 5 - 10 deep dive questions that test whether you are bullshitting. Write down the questions and the answers - or even better - incorporate your answers into your initial response.

■ CONCLUSION

Well done. You made it!

If you have filled in all these pages you are in a totally different place compared to when you started. You've thought, reflected and written.

You've spent hours and hours of preparation and you should have new found confidence as you go in to your interview process.

You should also have new found clarity.

If you have read it, worked through it all and secured a job - keep this book in a drawer for your next career move. If this book helped you, give it a review, share it on social media… or buy a copy for a friend or someone you are mentoring! Karma is cool… and you have a salary now!

Let me know how you get on - FISO* and don't get Filtered OUT!

Good luck!

Stay in touch…I share ideas and news on interviews, tech, storytelling, startups, leadership and business.

Connect with me on Twitter	@peterbotting
Follow me on LinkedIn	www.linkedin.com/in/peterbotting
Subscribe on YouTube	www.storytelling.expert

Thank You!

Peter

*You have to buy the other Filtered OUT book to find out what FISO means. Or go on the website…

Printed in Great Britain
by Amazon